BORN Wild
in COLORADO

WENDY SHATTIL and BOB ROZINSKI

FARCOUNTRY
PRESS

Above: When her fawn is about six weeks old, the mother mule deer will begin weaning it and introducing a diet of leaves, twigs, and some seeds and nuts.

Right: Red foxes are one of nature's most intelligent animals.

Title page: Twin mountain goats occur in about one-fourth of the species' births.

Front cover: Born to climb, this mountain goat kid is already practicing on its nanny's back.

Back cover, left: A mule deer fawn wanders through a Colorado grassland.
Back cover, right: Fox kits huddle together just outside their den.

ISBN: 978-1-56037-412-1

© 2007 by Farcountry Press
Photography © 2007 by Wendy Shattil and Bob Rozinski

For more information about our books, write Farcountry Press, P.O. Box 5630, Helena, MT 59604; call (800) 821-3874; or visit www.farcountrypress.com.

Produced and printed in the United States of America.

INTRODUCTION

by Wendy Shattil and Bob Rozinski

A mountain goat kid finds a tasty treat on a mountaintop.

Colorado remains a wild land of spectacular, varied habitats. From alpine tundra to shortgrass prairie, high mountain valleys to wetlands, the Centennial State is home to many of the iconic wild animals of the West.

Rocky Mountain National Park and Great Sand Dunes National Park and Preserve are havens for mule deer, elk, bighorn sheep, and moose. Most of Colorado's state parks, national wildlife refuges, and grasslands provide not only habitat but excellent access for wildlife viewing.

And among the most popular wild creatures to observe are birds. *Born Wild in Colorado* features the state's smallest bird, the broad-tailed hummingbird, as well as several of its largest, including sandhill cranes, white pelicans, and bald eagles.

Although many people venture out into Colorado's spectacular country to view these inspiring creatures, few have the opportunity to view wildlife young. This is why we are so honored to be able to present these images— rare and special moments of young creatures exploring their new world.

Encounters between humans and wildlife, however, are a major concern to wildlife experts. Even brief, well-intentioned interactions can be detrimental to animal babies. We have studied and observed wildlife for more than twenty-five years and use this knowledge to approach animals respectfully. We do not want to stress wildlife, and we go to great lengths to avoid disturbing babies. We believe that no photograph is worth jeopardizing an animal's safety. Therefore, we use the longest field lens available. It lets us photograph wild animals while maintaining a distance that does not alter the animals' behavior. Not only is this less stressful for our subject, but the distance allows the animal to behave naturally rather than react to us.

Some species are so elusive that they are rarely photographed in the wild. Cats such as mountain lions, lynx, and bobcats are rarely seen, particularly during the time when their young are born. We are fortunate to have access to hand-reared cats and photograph them in controlled situations—allowing people to gain an understanding of young creatures few ever see.

We prefer, however, to photograph wild animals in wild places, and every animal except the cats in this book was born in the wild. *Born Wild in Colorado* is the result of years spent in Colorado's varied habitats, watching wild animals where they live. We are thrilled to share our experiences and photographs with others.

Look for wildlife wherever you go in Colorado and discover for yourself the finest natural treasures the state has to offer.

Climbing trees is easy for black bear cubs. Unlike grizzlies, black bears retain this ability into adulthood.

Above: Porcupine pups are born with full sets of soft quills, which harden when exposed to the air. They can't actually throw their barbed quills; rather the hooked ends of the quills become embedded in the skin of animals that make contact with the porcupines.

Right: Broad-tailed hummingbirds typically nest in the same location year after year. They often return to the same branch and build a new nest on top of the old one. Nests are constructed of leaves, lichen, and bark and lined with plant down or spider silk.

Left: Juicy streamside plants are delicious treats for this white-tailed deer fawn.

Above: A bison yearling nimbly leaps over a creek. Bison can run as fast as thirty-five miles per hour.

Right: Beavers are Colorado's largest rodents. They have litters of four to five kits in the spring.

Facing page: This fuzzy gosling will one day be a majestic Canada goose that may migrate as far north as Alaska but may also stay in Colorado year-round.

Above: Three American badger kits hang out at the entrance to their burrow. Born in the spring, the kits leave home in the autumn of the same year.

Left: This striped skunk kit was probably born in a litter of four or five babies. Striped skunks are Colorado's most common type of skunk.

Facing page: For red fox kits and other wild babies, play-fighting and exploring help prepare them for adulthood.

Above: Tuckered out, a white-tailed deer fawn depends on its spotted coat to camouflage it while it naps in the tall grass.

Right: Startle an American bittern and it will point its bill up and hold perfectly still, seeming to become just another plant standing in the marshland.

Far right: The lynx, a larger relative of the bobcat, was reintroduced into Colorado in 1999.

Above: If this prairie dog mother spots a predator   a coyote, eagle, or badger—she'll alert her pups and the whole colony to dive into their burrows.

Left: Breakfast is served for an American white pelican chick, which is gobbling up the small fish its parent has scooped up and carried in its throat pouch.

Far left: Coyotes hunt all day long, but especially at dawn and dusk, and eat small mammals, birds, insects, and fruit.

Above: This deer mouse pup is fast asleep in its nest of fur and grass. Deer mice are so adaptable that they can live almost anywhere in North America, from deserts to pine forests.

Left: A velvety trumpeter swan chick is practicing its swimming. Trumpeter swans range from Alaska and Canada to the northwestern and north-central states, where they live on aquatic plants, insects, and invertebrates.

Above: Chickarees, also called red squirrels, are the forest's chatterboxes, scolding and teasing before scampering away through the treetops.

Right: The long legs of a moose allow it to wade into water for luscious plants and, in the winter, dig through the snow for food.

Facing page: A mountain lion cub cuddles with its mother in the warm sun. Colorado's foothills and canyons are home to these wild cats.

Above: These Rocky Mountain bighorn sheep triplets stick close to their mother as they graze in the high mountain terrain. Rocky Mountain bighorn sheep are native to Colorado. Their cousins, desert bighorn sheep, were introduced into Colorado National Monument, near Grand Junction, in 1979.

Facing page: Most mule deer are born in sets of twins from April through June.

Above: Two black-billed magpie fledglings balance on the branches outside their nest. Both parents continue to feed their fledglings for two or three months after they leave the nest.

Facing page: As this flammulated owl matures, the fuzzy fellow will develop rusty-red shoulder patches that extend along its wings. Its name means "reddish," or "flame-touched."

Above: Two pronghorn fawns follow their mother across a prairie. Prong-horns usually have twins, which weigh five to seven pounds each at birth.

Right: Cottontail bunnies, weighing about two pounds as adult rabbits, love brushy country for food and protective cover.

Far right: Curious coyote pups peer out from their den. They are born in litters of about six pups. The smallest of the three pictured is the "runt" of the litter.

Above: Golden-mantled ground squirrels look a little like chipmunks—except golden mantled ground squirrels have stripes on their back only, while chipmunks have stripes on their back and face. Both carry food home in cheek pouches.

Left: Despite their name, burrowing owls do not dig their own homes—they move into abandoned rodent burrows. Only nine inches tall as adults, they are migratory visitors to Colorado.

Above: A mountain plover chick ventures out into the shortgrass prairie surrounding its nest. The primary breeding ground for these birds, Colorado contains more than half of the world's population of nesting mountain plovers.

Right: A prairie dog mother and pup greet each other at the entrance to their home.

Facing page: Most bison calves are single births, starting out life at forty to fifty pounds. Within a couple of hours, they are able to run beside their mothers.

Above: Bald eagle chicks view the world from their large nest atop a cottonwood tree. Their parents took turns incubating the eggs for more than a month.

Left: This lynx kitten's paws will grow large for its body, which will help the animal move across deep snow while it searches for food in the winter.

Above: Is this swift fox practicing an intimidating posture or just yawning and stretching? Colorado's smallest foxes, the adults weigh just four to seven pounds and live on the eastern plains.

Right: Once these American dipper chicks leave the nest, they will forage in and near water for small fish, insects, and invertebrates.

Facing page: Taking a family stroll; it's hard to believe that these sandhill crane chicks will one day be about four feet tall like their parents.

Above: The Rocky Mountain bighorn sheep is Colorado's official mammal. These ewes exhibit the slightly curved spike horns of bighorn females; only the males develop huge, curled horns.

Left: Coyote pups are weaned at approximately seven weeks and then begin their young adult lives.

Facing page: Mountain lion cubs may look like domestic cats, but they will grow to weigh between 80 and 200 pounds, depending on their gender.

Above: Both parents have been feeding this nighthawk nestling with regurgitated food. When it is one month old, it will begin living on its own.

Right: This long-eared owl chick will grow to be thirteen to fourteen inches tall and will have large tufts on top of its ears, earning its name.

Far right: A trio of mountain goat kids plays on the rough slopes of the Rocky Mountains.

Above: Hungry Bullock's oriole chicks vie for a mouthful of regurgitated food from their mother. These birds reside in the western half of North America, choosing woodland, brushy, or riparian areas from Canada to Central America.

Left: A mallard duckling tests its beak on one of its siblings. Mallards begin to fly about two months after they have hatched. They will eat most anything that grows or lives in or at the edge of water—insects, seeds, small fish, and more.

Above: Is this bison cow guiding her calf back to the herd after it wandered off for some exploring?

Right: Three swift foxes strike an elegant pose for the camera.

Above: A clutch of eight burrowing owl chicks is unusual and a tribute to good parenting, plenty of food, mild weather, and few predators.

Left: From high atop the Colorado Rockies, a mountain goat kid surveys the rugged terrain.

Above: Mountain lion cubs are born with spots, which provide camouflage when they are ready to leave their den.

Right: Mallard chick siblings fall in line behind their mother for a swimming lesson.

Above: Long-tailed weasels, which live in many habitats throughout Colorado, have a tail that is about half the length of their body.

Left: Swift foxes' intelligence and complex social system—along with good speed for their small size—help make them very successful hunters.

Above: By the time winter arrives, this white-tailed ptarmigan chick will turn white to blend in with the snow, and its tufted feet will make perfect snowshoes.

Right: A striped skunk kit climbs atop a log for a better view.

Facing page: Black bear cubs are excellent climbers and, when mom's away, often take to the safety of trees.

Above: These broad-tailed humming-bird chicks will some day develop the shiny metallic green crowns and backs that characterize adults.

Left: Bison calves spend their first seven to twelve months being fed and defended by their mothers—which grow horns just as male bison do.

Facing page: Elk primarily eat grass; in the winter, they add twigs and bark to their diet.

Right: Moose cows aggressively defend their young, which are born in the spring. Twins are not uncommon, and calves are born with a reddish coat that darkens with age.

Below: As it matures, this curlew chick will grow a down-curving bill that helps it dig for insects in its shoreline habitat. For now, both parents are caring for it.

Above: Since black bears often den in hollow trees, this cub might be hanging out on its mother's front porch.

Left: A wild foal casts a sidelong glance as it grazes on the prairie. Today, an estimated 25,000 wild horses roam in the United States.

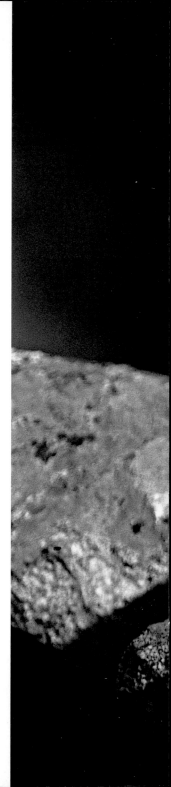

Above: A pair of mountain goat kids leaps from rock to rock.

Right: A baby marmot nuzzles its mother. Marmots are Colorado's largest ground squirrel, weighing about eleven pounds and measuring twenty-six inches long.

Left: A group of pronghorn does and fawns races across the prairie. Pronghorns are built for speed but not endurance—they can run as fast as sixty miles an hour in brief bursts in order to elude prey. They are the fastest animals in the western hemisphere.

Below: The black collar and white frame on its face indicate that this burrowing owl is maturing.

Above: A cottontail bunny warms itself in the sun on a frosty morning. Cottontail rabbits eat vegetation in the morning and evening, and hide in hollows in the ground during most of the day.

Right: For peregrine falcons, home-building is easy—they clean off a spot on a cliff's ledge and settle in. The parents mate for life and return to the same nesting spot each year.

Far right: A red fox kit licks leftover bits of food from its mother's muzzle.

Above: The thirteen-lined ground squirrel gathers meals consisting primarily of grass, seeds, caterpillars, and grasshoppers.

Left: When this great horned owl matures, it won't really have horns, but rather tufts of feathers rising from its ears. It will grow as large as twenty-five inches tall, with a wingspan of up to five feet.

Right: A sure-footed Rocky Mountain goat kid tests its legs amid the rocky crags.

Below: A young snowshoe hare drives forward as it speeds through a subalpine forest. Snowshoe hares are different than rabbits; hares are smaller and have larger hind feet that help them flee danger.

Above: Chattering at anything that interrupts its work, the American pika spends the summer harvesting grass and spreading it on rocks to dry for winter food.

Left: For the first week of its life, an eared grebe hitches a ride on the back of one of its parents and is fed by the other parent.

Above: Bobcats were so named because of their short tails, which look cut off or "bobbed." The adults grow to about three feet in length, with a tail only six inches long.

Right: When this moose calf grows up, it will grow a flap of skin, called a "bell," beneath its jaw. Moose are the largest members of the deer family, standing as much as six feet tall at the shoulder when fully grown.

Above: Bald eagles start life with dark-brown feathers and go through several color-changing phases before developing the white head and tail of an adult at four or five years old.

Left: Mountain goats' specialized body shape and hooves help them balance as they travel along narrow mountain ledges. Their cloven hooves spread apart for stability and the inner pads provide traction. Their dewclaws also help to prevent slipping.

Above: A baby marmot finds a comfortable spot on a rock. Marmots are most at home in rocky, mountainous areas and hibernate in the winter.

Right: The weasel is characterized by its long, narrow body and dark-colored back and white belly.

Above: Once spring's bright green fades to summer gold, a pronghorn's coat makes it invisible when it hides in the shortgrass prairie it favors.

Left: Both parents care for American coot nestlings like this one, and in turn, this nestling will help tend younger broods that are born later in the year.

Above: Wild horses roam Colorado's four unique wild horse herd management areas.

Right: When fully grown, this elk calf will weigh between 450 and 900 pounds.

Far right: Mom leads her two mule deer fawns through the tall grass.

Above: Two red fox kits enjoy some good-natured roughhousing.

Left: An elk cow and her calf are silhouetted by a fiery pre-dawn sky.

Wendy Shattil and Bob Rozinski

Although assignments have taken Shattil and Rozinski throughout North America, they spend most of their time photographing the Rocky Mountain West—particularly their home state of Colorado, where "a boundless supply of subjects will inspire us for a lifetime," says Wendy. They have photographed more of Colorado's wildlife than any other photographer or photographic team. Shattil's and Rozinski's award-winning camera work appears in hundreds of publications internationally and in twelve of their own books.

Wendy was the first woman awarded Grand Prize in the prestigious worldwide BBC Wildlife Photographer of the Year competition. The team received the Philip Hyde Grant for environmental photography, Denver Audubon's Environmental Stewardship Award, Conservationist of the Year, as well as Business of the Year Awards from the Colorado Wildlife Federation. They were research associates for the Denver Museum of Nature and Science and twice were artists in residence at Rocky Mountain National Park. Shattil and Rozinski were named Grand Prize winners in the Texas Valley Land Fund contest and First Prize winners in the *Nature's Best* international photography competition.